W9-ACK-223

21st Century Skills **INNOVATION** *Library*

Basketball

by Ellen Labrecque

INNOVATION IN SPORTS

Published in the United States of America by Cherry Lake Publishing
Ann Arbor, Michigan
www.cherrylakepublishing.com

Content Adviser: Matt Zeysing, Historian & Archivist, Naismith Memorial Basketball Hall of Fame

Design: The Design Lab

Photo Credits: Cover and page 1, ©iStockphoto.com/padnpen; pages 5 and 27, ©AP Photo; page 6, ©iStockphoto.com/gmcoop; page 9, ©iStockphoto.com/groveb; page 10, ©Joe Robbins; page 13, ©zimmytws, used under license from Shutterstock, Inc.; page 15, ©AP Photo/Grant Halverson; page 17, ©Jeff Greenberg/Alamy; page 18, ©David Durochik/Robbins Photography; page 20, ©Drazen Vukelic, used under license from Shutterstock, Inc.; page 23, ©AP Photo/Doug Pizac; page 25, ©AP Photo/Paul Vathis; page 28, ©AP Photo/Michael O'Brien

Library of Congress Cataloging-in-Publication Data
Labrecque, Ellen.
 Basketball / by Ellen Labrecque.
    p. cm.–(Innovation in sports)
 Includes index.
 ISBN-13: 978-1-60279-256-2
 ISBN-10: 1-60279-256-9
 1. Basketball–Juvenile literature. 2. Basketball–History–Juvenile
literature. I. Title. II. Series.
 GV885.1.L33 2009
 796.323–dc22   2008002044

Cherry Lake Publishing would like to acknowledge the work of
The Partnership for 21st Century Skills.
Please visit www.21stcenturyskills.org for more information.

CONTENTS

CHAPTER ONE

The Birth of Basketball

During the winter of 1891, James Naismith was a physical education instructor at the YMCA. The **bitter** cold days had arrived in Springfield, Massachusetts. It was too cold outside to play baseball or kick a soccer ball around the field. His students were starting to grow restless and bored. At first, Naismith had the students play outdoor games inside—such as soccer, lacrosse, and football. But windows and bones ended up getting broken. So Dr. Luther Gulick, the head of the physical education program at the YMCA, challenged Naismith to invent an indoor game that his students could enjoy. The 30-year-old gym instructor sat down at his desk and began to think.

Over the next several hours, Naismith came up with 13 rules for a new game. He decided that his game would

Dr. James Naismith invented the game of basketball.

be played with a soccer ball and two peach baskets that he found. The player with the ball was not allowed to move with the ball. Instead, the ball moved by passing. The peach baskets were attached to balconies at opposite ends of the court. The point of the game was to throw or "shoot" the ball into the basket to score a point. The team with the most baskets at the end of the game was declared the winner. Naismith took his 13 rules and posted them on a wall in the gymnasium. At first, when his students walked into the gym and saw the list, they weren't very excited.

"Hmmmmph!" one student groaned. "A new game!" But despite the students' lack of excitement, the game

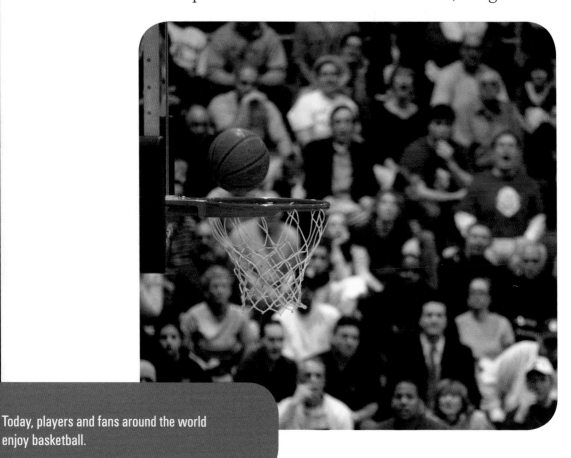

Today, players and fans around the world enjoy basketball.

became a huge hit. In the first matchup, the final score was 1–0. A boy by the name of William Chase scored the first basket, with a toss from 25 feet (7.6 meters) away.

"The only difficulty I had was driving [the students] out when the hour closed," Naismith said about the class that day.

The game spread like wildfire. At Christmas break, the boys in Naismith's class introduced the game at the YMCAs in their hometowns. Naismith also shared the rules with anybody who asked. Later that year, women teachers from an elementary school near the Springfield YMCA became the first females to play the game. The new sport was on its way to becoming one of the most popular on the planet.

Life & Career Skills

James Naismith was a modest man. If he weren't, basketball might have been named differently. Soon after the first game was played, one of Naismith's students pointed out that the sport needed a name. The student suggested "Naismith ball."

"That would kill any game," Naismith said with a laugh.

The student responded, "Why not call it basket ball?"

Naismith liked the sound of that. Basket ball it was. In 1921, the two words were combined into one—the name and sport were here to stay!

CHAPTER TWO

The Rules

The first basketball game—played with a soccer ball in a small gym—looked a lot different from the game today. Can you imagine LeBron James jamming a ball into a peach basket? The rules that have changed since that day in 1891 have made the sport faster and more exciting to play and watch! Even though the rules have changed, the spirit of the game remains the same.

Early in the game's history, fans continually got in the way of a player's shot. How could fans be kept from interfering in the game? Backboards were added to the game in 1894, and the problem was solved. Another early rule change came about because basketball players grew tired of passing the ball around all the time. Until 1896, players were not allowed to run with the ball. How could the game be made more active and exciting?

Dribbling is an important skill for anyone who wants to play basketball.

Dribbling! It was decided that a player could run with the ball as long as he bounced it up and down while he ran. Dribbling was introduced in 1896. Naismith called the addition of dribbling "one of the sweetest, prettiest plays in the whole bunch."

The exciting three-point shot is a recent innovation.

Fans soon became agitated with the low-scoring games. Players began thinking about how to fix the issue. In 1896, the value of a field goal was doubled from one point to two. This allowed higher scoring games and more excitement for fans. It wasn't until the 1979–80 season that the three-point shot was added to National Basketball Association (NBA) games. In 1986, the National Collegiate Athletic Association (NCAA) adopted the three-point shot as well. The long-range shot added some nail-biting fun to the game.

When the game was first established, nine players were on each team. This made the basketball court very crowded. Players were always bumping into each other. In 1905, it was decided that only five players were allowed on a team. This new rule helped unclog the court and made it easier for players to move.

Until 1906, somebody had to climb up a ladder and retrieve the ball after every shot that landed in the basket! Players grew tired of having to climb up to get the ball. The rules committee did something smart—they removed the bottom of the basket. Now the game moved more quickly.

Naismith had hoped basketball would not be a rough sport like football. But much to his annoyance, players realized a flaw in the rules. If they fouled a player every time he shot the ball, the shooter was granted only one free throw. In 1915, the "two-shot" rule was added in college basketball games. When a player was fouled, he was awarded two free throws worth one point each. This rule was enforced to **discourage** players from fouling one another. In 1923, another rule was added—free throws had to be shot by the player who was fouled, not just by the team's best shooter.

Learning & Innovation Skills

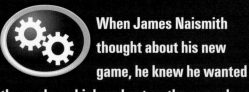 When James Naismith thought about his new game, he knew he wanted the goals up high and not on the ground. Why? In a sport such as football, a player can bulldoze his way into the end zone to make a touchdown. Naismith wanted scoring to take more finesse in his sport. He figured shooting a basket from far away would take skill, not just sheer will. Naismith secured the baskets to the lower rail of the balcony in the gym where he was teaching. The rail just happened to be exactly 10 feet (3 m) off the ground. Today, baskets are still set at exactly that height!

Players and fans still complained of games running too long or moving too slowly. What was causing the delays during basketball games? Basketball officials and players determined that the center jump after every shot was made was part of the problem. The center jump was **eliminated** after every shot in 1936. This helped the game flow more smoothly.

Additionally, the 24-second shot clock was invented in 1954. This meant the offense had to shoot within 24 seconds or give up possession of the ball. This rule prevented a team that was ahead in a close game from playing keep-away until the clock ran out. Today, NBA teams still get 24 seconds to take a shot, while college men get 35 seconds and college women get 30.

CHAPTER THREE

Basketball Equipment

Y ou don't need a lot of equipment to shoot some hoops. Players don't need pads or helmets or even cleats. When they show up to the court, they simply need a ball and a pair of sneakers.

When Naismith's class played that first game, they used a soccer ball. Over time, players felt that the game needed a ball of

A pair of athletic shoes and a basketball are all the equipment a basketball player needs.

its own. The sport didn't get one until 1929, when G. L. Pierce filed a **patent** for the "basketball." The ball was an outer shell of brown leather surrounding a rubber **sphere**. While Pierce's design was great for players, fans were having a tough time following the ball on the court. Tony Hinkle, the basketball coach at Butler University, invented the orange ball in the late 1950s. The bright orange ball immediately caught a fan's eye, making the game easier to follow.

Playing hoops is all about the footwear. Basketball shoes **evolved** from basic sneakers to the high-tech, high-price, high-style kicks that players wear today. Early in the game's history, players needed shoes that gave them support and flexibility. So in 1917, the Converse Rubber Shoe Company created the first "basketball sneaker"— just 25 years after the sport was invented. The "All-Star" sneakers were high-top brown canvas shoes with rubber soles. In 1921, basketball player Charles "Chuck" Taylor walked into the Converse offices searching for a job. He suggested using different material for more flexibility and support. He also suggested putting a patch on the shoes to protect a player's ankles. By 1923, the shoes were called Chuck Taylor All-Star shoes!

Today, the basketball shoe industry is a worldwide, billion-dollar business. Companies boast in advertisements that their shoes will help athletes jump

In 1921, basketball player Chuck Taylor suggested improvements to the Converse basketball sneaker. The shoes are still known as Chuck Taylor All-Stars.

INNOVATION IN SPORTS

Learning & Innovation Skills

 Just in time for the NBA's 2006–07 season, the league introduced a new ball. This new ball had a microfiber shell instead of the classic leather shell. The new ball was supposed to feel just like the old ones but would not wear as quickly. Sounds great, right? Wrong! Players found them way too slick. They complained about the ball's lack of grip. "It feels like one of the cheap balls that you buy in a toy store," said Shaquille O'Neal.

Just because something is new doesn't mean that it is better. And it is important to accept feedback and act on it. That's what the NBA did. Much to the relief of players, the league brought back the old ball on January 1, 2007.

higher and run faster. Athletic shoe companies such as Reebok and Nike pay athletes to wear their shoes. Allen Iverson has a contract with Reebok estimated at $5 million a year for life! LeBron James has a shoe contract with Nike reportedly worth $13 million a year. So, how much does a pair of Allen Iverson or LeBron James shoes cost? Iverson's Answer XI retails at $99.99. A pair of James's Nike Zoom LeBron IV is sold for the bargain price of $150! These expensive shoes may not make you a star, but at least you'll look cool while you're playing!

CHAPTER FOUR

Training to Win

Today, serious players must do more than simply shoot hoops in their driveway. A player who wants to become a star has to attend basketball camps, watch instructional videos, and do dribbling and shooting drills every day. Training to play basketball, even as early as the grade-school level, can be a full-time job!

Many young basketball players sign up for summer basketball camps to work on their skills.

Kobe Bryant is one of basketball's great shooters.

Shooting is one aspect of the game that has evolved into an art form. When the game first began, players launched the ball from beneath their legs with two hands. Today, shooters release the ball from behind their head, using one hand to launch the ball and the other to **precisely** guide it. Becoming a great shooter takes practice, practice, and more practice. Los Angeles Lakers' star Kobe Bryant claims he made, not just shot, 100,000 baskets in one summer. "I don't practice taking shots," Bryant said. "I practice making them."

Dribbling is another aspect of the game that requires endless hours of practice. Watch an NBA or college game, and you'll see players dribble the ball at lightning speed with ease and grace. These players most likely spent hours every day dribbling in their driveways and at their local gyms.

Life & Career Skills

Kobe Bryant is one of the best players in the history of the game. In December 2007 at age 29, he became the youngest NBA player to reach 20,000 points as a pro. He has been named to 10 NBA All-Star teams and helped the Los Angeles Lakers win NBA titles in 2000, 2001, and 2002. It's no wonder he's the best. Bryant is also one of the hardest workers in the game. He knows how much training it takes to be the kind of player he is.

During the off-season, Bryant wakes at 5:30 AM to work out. He eats five times a day—only healthy foods such as fruits and vegetables. He spends hours watching and learning from game tapes of past and present players. He also spends hours running distances and doing sprint work.

"I work extremely hard," Bryant said. "I take all the steps and do all the work necessary. I'm not going to cheat the game."

Working out with weights is an important part of many basketball players training plan.

Legendary point guard Bob Cousy helped lead the Boston Celtics to six NBA titles in the 1950s and 1960s with his amazing dribbling skills. He was the first to perfect the behind-the-back dribble. Opponents called Cousy "a magician." But he didn't see anything magical about his skills. He just practiced a lot.

The game has gotten faster and faster throughout the years. Edgar A. Diddle, a coach at Western Kentucky for 42 seasons (1922–1964), is the pioneer of fast-break basketball. He pushed his team to play the game at breakneck speed and often exhausted his opponents into defeat. Coach Paul Westhead, who led the Los Angeles Lakers to the 1980 NBA title, is also one of the game's most **avid** speed demons.

This "need for speed" means basketball players have to be in better shape than ever before. Players train with weights, eat special diets, and spend hours doing running and sprinting drills. But this doesn't mean shooting and other skills can be pushed to the sidelines. Players just have to learn to do these skills faster. Let's learn about some famous players who not only trained hard to become the best, but changed the way the game is played.

CHAPTER FIVE

Basketball Greats

Basketball's history is filled with dunks, dribbles, and magical moments. Along the way, these four people helped mold the game into the high-flying, heart-stopping spectacle it is today.

Kareem Abdul-Jabbar—The Hero of the Hook

In 1956, Ferdinand Lewis Alcindor Jr. shot his first "sky-hook" as a fifth-grader. Little did he know just how successful the sky-hook would be during his career.

Alcindor changed his name to Kareem Abdul-Jabbar in 1971. But he never changed his most famous shot— the sky-hook. Using this shot, he helped UCLA win three straight NCAA titles (1967–69). As a pro, he led the Los Angeles Lakers to five NBA titles in the 1980s. When he retired in 1989, no NBA player had ever scored

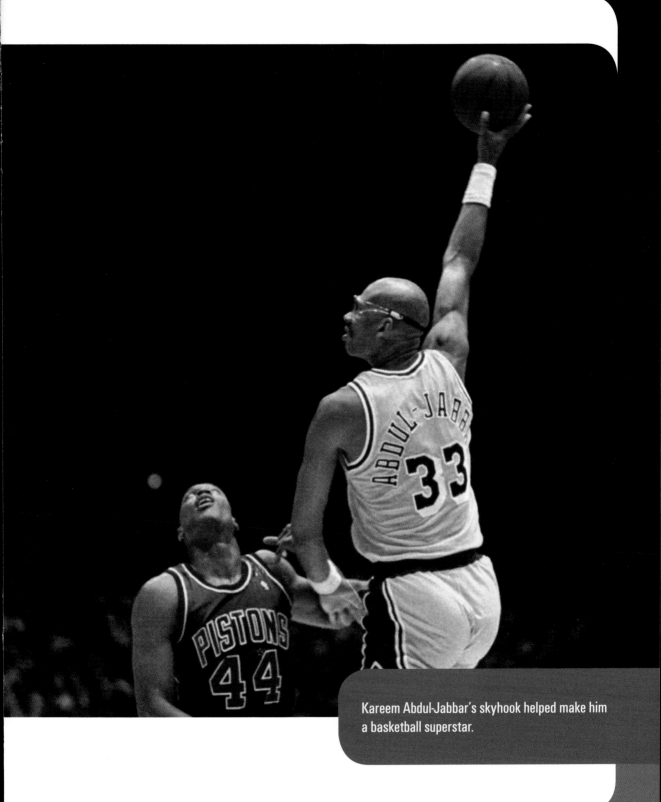

Kareem Abdul-Jabbar's skyhook helped make him a basketball superstar.

more points or blocked more shots than Kareem. "Let's toast him as the greatest player ever," said Pat Riley, who coached Kareem for eight seasons as a Laker.

The sky-hook was **virtually** undefendable. At 7 feet 2 inches (2.18 m), Kareem would extend his right arm over his head and snap his wrist, looping the ball toward the net. The shot usually ended with a swish. The only way to block the ball was to jump up and over him—which was next to impossible. "You could have fallen out of the ceiling and never blocked the shot," said Nate Thurmond, a former NBA center. The sky-hook made Kareem Abdul-Jabbar one of the most **dominant** athletes in the game.

Wilt Chamberlain—The Rule Changer

Center Wilt Chamberlain was so good that he changed the way the game was played. During his college and pro careers (1956–73), rules were added because of his dominant play.

For example, the rules stated that a player could not stay in the lane for more than three seconds. Because of his height, the 7-foot-1 (216 cm) Chamberlain simply straddled the narrow lane. He forced the rules committee to widen the lane from 8 feet (2.4 m) to 12 feet (3.7 m). The NBA lane is now 16 feet (4.9 m). Another change he inspired regarded shooting a free throw. Chamberlain

Wilt Chamberlain holds up a sign reading "100" after his record-setting performance against the New York Knickerbockers in 1962.

was able to take off from the foul line and reach the basket. So the rules committee outlawed dunking free throws. Lobbing the inbound pass over the backboard to another player also became illegal. Why? Chamberlain simply jumped up and dunked the pass. His **prowess** made players and officials rethink the way the game was played.

Chamberlain's most famous mark on the game occurred on March 2, 1962. He scored 100 points in one game. His team, the Philadelphia Warriors, beat the New York Knicks, 169–147. He shot 36-for-63 from the field. After the game, he had only this to say: "That's terrible. I never thought I'd take that many shots in a game."

Dr. Julius Erving—Man in Flight

Before Kobe, before LeBron, even before superstar Michael Jordan, there was Julius "Dr. J" Erving. He was one of the first players to play above the rim. He played 11 seasons with the Philadelphia 76ers (1976–87) and led them to the NBA crown in 1983. He averaged 22 points per game during his NBA career.

Dr. J was simply a wizard in the air. He propelled himself up like a helicopter in flight, defying gravity with 360-degree spins. He usually finished with a powerful slam-dunk or a delicate finger roll.

In his most famous move, Dr. J drove past a defender along the right baseline. He then jumped into the air as he approached the side of the backboard. Another defender blocked his journey to the rim. So Erving brought the ball back down but kept his body afloat behind the backboard, seemingly forever, to the other side of the hoop. There he put up a soft, underhanded scoop for the score. This legendary move became known as the "baseline move."

Julius Erving was one of the first basketball players to play above the rim.

Nancy Lieberman—The Girl Has Game

Back in the early 1900s, women played basketball in dresses and high heels. Today, women dress just like the men—in shorts and jerseys. But more important, the women play the game just as fast and furiously as their male counterparts. Nancy Lieberman, who played college and pro basketball in the 1970s and 1980s, is a big reason why this is the case. "Lady Magic" led Old

Nancy Lieberman was known for her tough play and determination on the court.

Dominion University to back-to-back national titles in 1979 and 1980 with her spot-on shooting and brilliant passing. The 5-foot-10-inch (178 cm) guard played in various women's professional leagues after college. Lieberman's biggest impact to the sport came when she proved skilled enough and tough enough to join the Springfield Fame of the United States Basketball League in 1986. She became the first woman to play in a men's professional league.

"It's beyond my expectations," Lieberman said about the popularity of the women's game today. "The overall quality continues to improve. Thanks to the young players, the game is in good hands."

21st Century Content

Basketball became an Olympic sport in 1936. Since then, the game has grown in popularity around the world. Take a look at the following numbers to see how popular the game has become:

350 million: People worldwide who played some organized version of basketball in 1991, the game's 100-year anniversary

450 million: People worldwide who played some organized version of basketball in 2007

Glossary

avid (AV-id) enthusiastic

bitter (BIT-ur) intensely unpleasant

discourage (diss-KUR-ij) to attempt to keep someone from doing something

dominant (DOM-uh-nuhnt) having the most power or control of a situation

eliminated (ih-LIM-uh-nate-id) to get rid of

evolved (ih-VOLVED) to develop gradually

finesse (fih-NESS) skill in action or performance

microfiber (MY-kroh-fye-bur) a very thin, usually soft, polyester fiber

patent (PAT-uhnt) the sole right granted by a government to an inventor to make, use, or sell an invention

precisely (prih-SYSE-lee) definite or exact

prowess (PROU-iss) exceptional or superior ability

sphere (SFEEHR) a rounded body or mass

virtually (VUR-choo-uh-lee) for the most part, almost wholly

For More Information

BOOKS

Basketball. New York: DK Publishing, 2005.

Fleder, Rob, ed. *Sports Illustrated: The Basketball Book*. New York: Time Inc. Home Entertainment, 2007.

Stewart, Wayne. *A Little Giant Book: Basketball Facts*. New York: Sterling Publishing, 2007.

WEB SITES

Naismith Memorial Basketball Hall of Fame
www.hoophall.com
For biographies of members of the Hall of Fame, including players, coaches, and more

Naismith Museum and Hall of Fame
www.naismithmuseum.com
Learn more about basketball's inventor, James Naismith

The Official Web Site of the National Basketball Association
www.NBA.com
Includes information on current and former players

Index

About the Author

Ellen Labrecque is a freelance writer living in northern New Jersey. Her other books include *Magic Johnson* in the Life Skills Biographies series and *Running* in the Healthy for Life series. Previously, she was a reporter and editor for eight years at *Sports Illustrated Kids* magazine.